Never Been Here Before

BOOKS BY THOMAS TIMMINS
www.thomastimmins.com

Novels
> *The Hour Between One and Two (Trilogy)*
>> *Blood Medicine*
>> *The Special Fruit Company*
>> *Down at the River*
> *Aphrodisiac for an Angel*

Short Fiction
> *Puff of Time*
> *Visions of My Other Self*
> *Desert Dusk Music*
> *The Silence of Frogs (Illustrated)*

Graphic Verse Novel
> *Zom*

Poetry
> *Likings for Shadows*
> *I Was Just Laughing*
> *Food Breaks Free*
> *Almost Everyone*
> *some say yes*
> *Never Been Here Before*
> *between worlds*
> *card tricks*

Never
Been Here
Before

POEMS

Thomas Timmins

Never Been Here Before © 2020 Thomas Timmins
All rights reserved.

ISBN: 978-0-9975112-5-3

Published by Zoëtown® Media
Zoëtown is registered trademark of Zoëtown Media.
Greenfield, MA
www.thomastimmins.com

Book and cover design by Maureen Moore,
Ginger Cat's Booksmyth Press
www.thebooksmythpress.com

For Amy

List of poems

Section I Faking it

"I", "I", "I"

Do you read poetry?
Or listen to it read?
Or write poetry yourself?
Or never feel the slightest interest in poetry?

Then you know
so many poems say
"I" did this,
"I" saw that,
"I" felt something.

Even when the poem says "you",
it often means "I".

Can you guess why?

It has to do
with the eyes in our heads.

Speaking with others, flesh or metal or plastic

Perhaps we won't speak about them
as people wanna-be's but as themselves.

Maybe we'll do that as soon as they tell us their names.
In the meantime, we'll address them as "friend."

Side by side, standing on grass with shovels and spades
in our hands, inside with our fingers on the keyboards,
or hanging out, we'll speak our given names as "friend."

Deep down, we enjoy hearing and speaking the word
"friend" when it refers to the real us and the real others.

If the others respond to us with "friend," we'll all be fine,
if anonymous from each other.

And if you want, you can address me as "Friend Tom."
Anytime, anywhere, for real.

You say "we"

You say "we"
when you mean "I."
It doesn't bother me,
I won't cry.

As long as we can walk
in pain, or not,
let's listen, let's talk,
if you want, we can brew a pot.

This morning, as ever,
I got up then sat down to work.
You called, said, Why don't you come over?
I just put the coffee on to perk.

It's the oldest tale.
Who cares if we forget to pick up the mail.

Beats in time

I can never get lonesome
enough to stop worrying about
how much is enough and
the conditions and qualities
worldwide
of potable water in 2035, or even 2025,
especially at the end of
summer when every cricket
and locust in the Northern Hemisphere
calls out in shadows, practicing their graduation
speeches to other Insect Toastmasters
and crooning to their paramours
until every conscious creature in the woods
with ears has memorized them.
The most common theme is
"We're all in these weeds together
so why don't we sing till dawn?"
I check my battery-driven Timex travel clock,
its ticky beat counter-pointing the bug harmonies.
I count seconds using my
my clock to calculate tomorrow's temperature,
its battery a secure promise to endure
blackouts, brownouts, shakeups of the night-
time electricity grid. No need
for a weather app
when the clock ticks
and the crickets chirp.

Never been here before

Everywhere I go these days,
I've never been here before.

Like waking up on the first morning
of a camping trip into the mountains
or climbing out of a train
and emerging in a city
I've never visited,

I'm always arriving at a new place.
I'm always moving and moving through a world
I could never imagine.

At the same time, I'm stopped like a boat
anchored in the middle of a windy lake.

Everywhere I look,
I've never seen this before
and I don't care.

I can identify some sounds -
breeze bumping through trees,
high squeals I know are voices.

I recognize my children
but they smell like no one I've ever hugged.

I know my hands
like I know birch trees
but how white they are surprises me.

And the memories of a boy named Tommy
and his mom and the blue bicycle he found
in the basement of a new house in a new town -
they're familiar.

But today's blue sky and the square buildings
and muddy cars and soft ground underfoot
almost make me laugh, they're so odd.

It's spring
after a dull, dark, gloomy dragged-out winter.
I may be seeing the same old things
and don't recognize everything
and I don't care because
my heart pumps with happiness
at seeing its old friend
the light.

"The Source"

What matters then

What matters then
now the roof broke through, hens ran off, too.
What matters now is the hank of lace
I snipped from mother's wedding gown.

And what could matter more
than the lads finding the work they love
and the girls the love they work.

What matters then blown down the street,
the torn snapshot of naked baby Madeline
with her mom and dad the day of her baptism.

And now, what matters is the curl
in what's left of Monte's hair and the bow
in Maria's apron hanging ten dry years
on the pantry hook, in memoriam.

Time pieces

The face of the inmate's watch,
propped at a right angle to the table,
tells the correct digital time
in customary chartreuse numbers
that lurch ahead once every minute
grazing across a twenty-four hour map of the day,
the same day every day,

while its red second needle
and its luminous minute and hour hands
freeze at the analog moment of
seven forty nine and thirty nine seconds,

rusted gates posted on each side of the day
that guide the digital herds
into the corral of every morning
and into the meadows of dreams of every night.

Infinite sweetness

Where the statue of the Blessed Virgin
once rose before the bent heads of
stiff Sunday-coiffed women,
now a red glass heart lay gleaming,
tilted on its side, its pulse stilled,
as if exhausted
by too much compassion,
answering too many prayers,

asking for its own miracle,
an instant transformation
into a giant cherry Valentine-shaped lollipop
people could help themselves to,
licking until she disappeared
into a memory of infinite sweetness.

Back porch blues

"Don't be sad for me"
Macy Gray

Down here in the cellars of reality
the wheezy singer warbles out
"Don't no body fret for me
I ain't no body who wants to shout
Nothin but the truth
so Don't feel sad for me"

She's for real
and what a deal
but who's this lad with his feet propped up
leanin on the railin
lookin over the swampy pond
of his imagination where cow lilies shine
his head kicked back in shock
Or is he laughin at a dream
of a green baby whose necklace read his name
his fingertips steepled in prayer to the only god
he could count on both hands
The god he met only by the inference of adrenaline
the dawn he wrapped his Chevy
around the mighty sycamore
the hangin tree not so many years ago in the nights
of drunken hounds rollin around
in the ecstasy of bloody ivy
whose muddy leaves today wind in and out

of the lattice under the very porch where he sits
grinnin at just how much he can take
because if he don't
the rest of them will just ignore the groans
and the past will disappear
like they want it to
unless he opens his palms to spikes of light
careless caresses he'll let spill into the world
one day when he learns to give his love
without the dread, without the shame
No body feelin sad for no body
Nothin doin but watchin the wind
blow ripples down the pond

Summer hoops at the keloid cliffs

Tonight on the outdoor court,
shooting baskets at the foot of the keloid cliffs
just before sunset, the long scar
crawling down the center of my chest,

my chest naked in the desert heat,
muscles stiffening against the
stretching and snapping of tendons and ligaments,
more used to quivering in service of
fingertips at the keyboard
than shooting hoops,
and my lungs, my lungs
baked to their mineral elements
and my round belly
visible to everyone,

everyone who happened to be
two middle school girls,
both blonde, sisters maybe, aunt
and niece? the older one a large girl,
and the svelte younger one, who caught
my errant ball as it rolled across
the schoolyard lawn,
and bounced it back to me,
my only witnesses,

13

as they ignored me
in favor of one of the swings
the younger one
sat down on squealing
while the older one pushed,

and my shots – ah, i finally
loosened up – dropped again and again
through the chain net
until after a while I got bored,
tucked the ball under my arm,
picked up my shirt and phone
with my smudged hands
and ambled toward my car,

leaving the girls the privacy
of their own company
though they most likely didn't care
one way or the other

anywhere near as much as I cared
about still putting up a few shots,
remembering how i was once good,
now ten years after I keeled over on the court
waking up in an oxygen mask,
a good way to go
I imagined later,
proud of taking with joy
the last pass on the fast break

14

to the next world
but, lucky me, failing to score
the fatal shot that night,
leaving heaven to the saints

as I came back to this world
so I could toss a few more shots
through the nets
for as many more years
as I still can
until I fire up my last three ball,
and watch the final swish
from the free throw line,
and feel the last kiss off the glass
of the perfect layup
at the buzzer.

Introducing me to Oona

for Oona and Danny

On the corner of Stanton and Orchard
everyone but her
was jawbone to cellphone,
even her boyfriend
who called his father
who lived far off in the desert,
and at the same time he pulled out
his wallet to buy her a slice
of pizza.
She heard the father's
laugh half-bark out of her
boyfriend's ear
when he spelled her name
for the old man.
A two-syllable name
meaning
"The one."
When her boyfriend
clicked his phone
shut, she asked
"Why did he laugh?"
"He was happy.
I'm happy," he said,
snagging a fine
string of cheese from her chin.

Grinning, he tipped his head
back, and he laughed again,
slid the fine line of cheese
between his lips, and
he laughed again.
Now she started laughing.

Arsa longa, vitae brevis

As once-upon-a-time Catholic poet
Ted Berrigan said,
writing poetry's 'taking the vows.'

Keeping his vows
and taking his bows
at a higher price than
any bishop's
emerald-, ruby- and diamond-inlaid
golden chalice –
Berrigan sacrificed his liver
on the altar of the page.
He died at 48.

He lay in bed with his wife and kids,
his body bloated by his speed-wrecked kidneys,
a Manhattan narwhal stranded
with mate and cubs in an icy corner
two bedrooms above a pizza shop
on East 5th Street.
Bearded and gray, yet still a grinning boy,
he stares up at the camera.

In his eyes,
the vows,
the sacramental pledge

to write and write and write
his death poem
if it's the last thing
he ever does.
He 'll write sonnets.
He'll write songs.
He'll write novels.

Ted Berrigan will
write and write and write ....

never hopeless,
welcoming the night.

Arsa longa, vita brevis.
Art is long. Life is short,
the first lines of a medical text by
Hippocrates. It goes on:
Opportunity is fleeting,
experimentations perilous,

**Can
dle
light
flick
er
ing**

Two flames rising together
can light up corners with
glow and with gentle fingers
empty pockets of gloom and
reveal remarkable things
wavering in distances one
candle burning alone can
never reach. Two candle
flames glimmering across
a table or across a bed soften
the shadows bending around,
but do not banish them. Yet,
a single flame, a tear of light,
a bright streaming of vapor
into the surrounding dark,
its ardent tongue tolling
notes of the song of grace,
its inner heat carried away
to total loss in the air –
a flame alone mirrors the gift
at the source: our reckless sun.

The financial power of political poetry

Donald Trump offered me a million dollars
to write a poem about him.

I said, No way. I won't compromise
my values to write a poem
for someone who has no heart,
a damaged brain,
a hating and cruel and hurtful mind
who's afraid of poetry
because it speaks the truth,
as well as it can.

How about 5 million, he said.

No way, I said. Money doesn't mean
much to me. I'm an artist.

Artists gotta live, too, he said.
Here's my last offer: 10 million.

Who said poets couldn't negotiate.
With 10 million, I could do all kinds
of good things. So I said OK
and wrote this.

"DT is DT.
He is who he is.
You know who he is.
He doesn't care about
anyone but himself
and his hairdresser.
Not his wife, his kids,
certainly not anyone
who doesn't suck up
to him or comes from
the wide world
where life is different
and fragile.
DT is DT.
He does what he wants
and to hell with
anything or anybody else."

I sent him the poem
and an invoice
for $10 million,
due upon receipt.

That was 8 months ago.
I didn't hear a word
until yesterday when
I got a call
from the Department of Justice.

The voice on the phone said
I owed the president
12 million dollars for the time
he spent negotiating
with me. The lawyer said
he liked your poem
and is going to use it
someday. So he'll deduct
the $10 million.
If you don't pay him
$2,000,000 in 30 days,
you can expect a knock
on your door
from one of our guys.

I'm pretty nervous
but I'm happy
because it shows
how poems can be powerful
and worth millions of dollars.

I don't know what
will happen to me.
Just so you don't worry,
I bought a book called
How to disappear
and now, I'm out of here.

No phone, no internet anything.
This is my penultimate poem

The last poem I write
will be for Elizabeth Warren.
I'll write it for free
under whatever name
I'm using at the time.

It will start
"Elizabeth,
Here's a $100 dollars,
my poet's lifetime earnings.
You care about us."

Sometimes we let the words

Sometimes we let the words
reveal
what we mean,
sometimes we say
directly
what we mean,
sometimes nobody
understands
the words
and sometimes
that's when we
come the closest
to knowing
anything at all.

Meditations on the "I"

The ones behind the "I" live in smiles that know.

Longing lingers as a reminder of endless change.

Tomorrow's people walk with love and desire
          beyond hope.

Perseverance and meditation, roots and wings,
          pouring and drinking.

A dance tune can scramble the stodgy "I".

◆◆

The "I"'s have dark eyes,
the eyes shed the tears,
the tears overflow
washing away the dust on the cheeks
clearing the vision so
"I" can see you weeping, too,
in the sunlight streaming
through the curtains,
while your chest rises and falls
in the same slow rhythm
as waves washing the shore
from a windless sea.

What is it?

It looks like love
& feels like love
& smells like love
& tastes like love
& sounds like love
but it's probably not
music
or poetry.

It's like pottery.
When you drop it from high,
it will shatter.
When you drop it from low,
when you're lucky,
it will bounce.

Sensory overload

Forgive me, children.
I didn't know
that energy
is not all.

The spark,
the blast,
the flood of
light and noise -

as if an action film
played endlessly
from long ago bang
to eternal boom,

all living bodies,
all rock,
all matter
buried in the sky,

hidden or known,
out of mind,
or here
in hand,

burning,
swirling like smoke,
changing shape,
chasing empty space,

filling the future
with roars,
crying out
its name,

touching
its flame
into dark
nothing,

dragging its past,
the glow of debris
sprayed across
its trail,

a gleam of something made,
time in a jumble,
its own past
the audience,

inert,
mirror-eyed,
bored
with the same old thing.

So to wake itself up,
to give its tail
its money's worth,
the energy

poured farther away,
splashed chaos
into virgin silence,
starred

the heavens
with bigger,
louder
bangs,

until even I,
faithful watcher,
cryer of cosmic rain,
awed mimic

of power,
capped devotee of energy,
applause for unflagging
performance,
became sated
with light, color,
sound, possibility,
and began to snore

when I could have
sat on the floor
playing blackjack
with the kids.

Green hand, painting by Bill Tierney, Santa Barbara, CA

Longing fulfilled

Truth   We have a large old house
               in a small town.

Gratitude   Autumn light floods the yard
               with its ragged shrubs
               and anarchic maples,
               twelve-foot sunflowers,
               sprawling lilacs,
               rampant raspberries,
               and all the neighborhoods' children.

Energy We're not careful gardeners
               but we seed our land with abandon.

Not Kids   Will the same be true
               when your hair grays and coarsens?

The Yard   Let it grow.

We Do Age   And when we hunch and shuffle?

Older   The question
               holds its own answer.
               Love, fragrant and moist,
               bears its fruit in the season
               of lengthening night.

Dream After us, when the town is gone,
             black bear will explore this yard,
             berries their prey,
             in this same honey-gleam of light.

David

I saw your handsome mug today in a photo
in the brochure Non-Violent Peace Force
sent to donors and would-be donors like me.
You looked pale, bro, standing beside the helicopter

with a friend, ready to depart, wearing a dark slouch hat
under the South Sudan sun. Maybe from too much light,
maybe too much violence everywhere you try and try
to make non-of.

You were smiling your ambivalent smile, the one
I first saw on your face when they'd tossed
your young radical self decades ago into the hoosegow,
then poured more drugs into you than you'd ever take

yourself. It's your smile that says, "Yeah,
this is a big deal, but it's nothing really."

Gentle grace

Sometimes
when something common,
like water, surrounds us
we feel surprised

at how calm
the day looks,
how smoothly
the waves flow
past our faces.

Sometimes,
when something
approaches us,
something startling
we can recognize,

something like love,
but we can't name it
because we don't know
we only feel

some gentle grace
lighting up
like sunlight after rain,
a peacefulness
everywhere in our bodies

and we surprise ourselves
with how we feel
at home.

Her accent

A few booths over, in the Subway restaurant,
where I sat among men in t-shirts
who stopped in for lunch like me – maybe
grilled chicken sub with hot peppers
and chipotle sauce, some lettuce,
a few tomatoes, so we could tell our wives
we ate a healthy lunch –

a short, thin Chinese woman
sitting in a booth next to me
with a handsome teenage boy,
abandoned her food and the boy and
marched out the door with her phone
in hand. She was heard calling out

in a loud fast voice, speaking English
with a lilt and a happy beat of someone
who was born and raised elsewhere.

Spelling, counting

He used to be so proud
he could spell anything
until words like
"scofflaw" and "odyssey"
seemed to belong
to another language
that was too hard
or too late to learn.

He never spoke them aloud anyway,
so why should he bother
to spell them the way
the online dictionary did,
much less remember
what they meant.

"Subsistence"
"Prosyletize"
"Raiment"

He found it easier to
add, subtract, multiply, divide.
He didn't have to remember how.
The answers just came.
Lately, he'd stop caring if
the numbers were right or wrong.
Close enough, he'd say.

Too Much

Yes, too much.
Too much pleasure, too much closeness,
too much talk, too many questions, too much told,
too much time together, too much time apart,
too much happiness, too much history,
too many responsibilities, too much possibility,
too many losses,
too much love, too many miles apart,
too many people, too much anger unspent,
too much light, too much warmth,
too much longing, too many hours not sleeping,
too much too soon, too much too late,
too much love, too many kisses, too much skin,
too many eyes, too many years apart, too long long ago,
too much rash, too few touches, too much fever,
too many shadows, too many questions,
too much laughing, too few tears,
too hot, too fast, too many paths,
too many thoughts, too little time,
too old, too young, too weak, too strong,
too high, too real, too false,
too this, too that, three or more
dance on the floor, three or less
we must confess to too many of us,
too late to stop
to ever be enough ....

Overheard at the movies

I can't tell you what had happened
because it didn't happen to me.
It happened at the movies
if it happened anywhere.

You were there
and so was I –
nights like those
we don't forget.

We heard her say from the row in front of us
"It took me 12 years to get over him.
What's hard for me
right now, always, is bearing the past."

We shook our heads, smiled, leaned over,
kissed each other. Kissed again.

One Month after the Separation

Crippled as I feel at the town's edge,
forgetting the name of translucent red
and blue shiny berries that end up as
pink birdsplotch on windshields,

I run limping through my own belly.
How will my sons miss me?
After Sparky, my dog love of childhood,
was crushed by a pickup driver,
I locked myself in my room, crying
all night. I never loved another dog,
or wanted one.

O, they're still mowing yards in Kansas.
Odors of chopped chlorophyll waft into
the oaks, brushing brittle leaves
like shadows of long fallen acorns.

The Tale of the Upside Down Man and the Woman Without Bones

Born with an upside down heart
he felt everything backwards.

When others cried, he laughed.
When others sighed, he shouted out.

He never smiled when he was pleased
or groaned when the pain hit hard.

When he stood on his head
or walked on his hands

he felt euphoric
as if walking on air.

So he joined the traveling circus
and worked in its Freak Show.

"The Upside Down Man" could dance a jig,
twirl and do flips on one bare hand or both.

His feet shaped and spoke in silent words,
his brick red face shone bright.

He wore his hair long in a ponytail
with blinking colored lights woven in.

He whipped his hair into lightning
on the darkened stage. The audience cheered.

For extra money, he let his fans
touch the callouses on his palms.

Then he fell in love with the beautiful performer
in the next tent – "The Woman Who Has No Bones."

She had bones, only she could contort her body
into almost any shape the audience wanted.

She refused to twist or flex into any ribald poses
and had the bouncer remove any perverts.

The Woman Who Had No Bones was an illusionist
whose voice cloaked the audience with sleepy calm.

She would form a rocket ship, growl take-off noises
and the audience would see fire and smoke

or, depending her whim, she'd shape a lily
so the audience could swoon in its heady fragrance.

When she met the Upside Down Man,
they laughed and agreed it was easy to fool the audience.

It took no more than a few hand and foot holdings
and a pretzeling hug before they fell in love.

They married and slept toes to heads.
She warmed his feet, he cuddled her toes.

Their favorite meals were finger foods
and spaghetti, their favorite number was 69.

They felt sad together when she sobbed
and he laughed so hard he cried.

When they were happy,
they kissed each other's feet.

Time, people, things

We don't think about time
the way the old ones did,
back before the beginning of clocks.

Pages we've always had,
slots of events and numbers, static reports
we could always refer to, even years later.

(By we, I mean us people,
the species in control here,
or, really, the one believing so.)

Most agree our time today feels cluttered
and slippery like in a dream
but when we're wide awake.

We don't want to
but we slide down endless time,
most of us dropping off too soon.

Some drag their feet,
some cling to things resisting
surrender to the end of time.

The moral lesson of time might be simple:
Cling to people as we slide to feel
comfort and inspiration in their arms,

while our things sneak off and fade away
and we don't really miss them
except when we remember what they meant to us

and when we reminisce about them
as we regale each other about our lives,
and that's quite something, isn't it?

Cinders

Again it's come time
to celebrate the end
of the dark days of the calendar
while again letting pass
the dark days of humans
who ignore the clock
because time means nothing
to them who fear the light.

Among many of us
who are stained by
our losses and ignorance,
we've missed offering kindness
to others in early morning
or in the dappling of noon
or at the edges of night.

Instead, we're known,
no matter the season,
to kindle flames again and again
and stare into the flickerings,
inhaling the fragrant smoke
that rises half shadow, half starry sky,
until we close our eyes
on the glowing cinders
for a while, finally relaxed.

After a while, we rouse ourselves,
mumble good night
and feel our way
into the night.

Bear's Den

Townsfolk call it
Bear's Den
to make us think back
to the wild times
before the woods
surrounding the tall cliffs
became a town park.

Not a place to stay,
it's too close to town,
and it's hard to find
unless, following hearsay,
you already searched it out.

These days, the bear live
down by the river
leaving the cave
for human children
to discover
and scramble up to,
excited, scared a little
by the cave's name.

Here's the map:
Follow the common trail
south until you curve left uphill

and hike north along the base
of the granite cliff.

If you spot a shadow
hidden partway up
by brambles, branch litter,
criss-crossed fallen trunks,
you'll know it's a good cave
because it's easy
to approach and hard
to climb up to.

Inside, some summers
you'll find a ragged
and soggy sleeping bag,
a homeless retreat.
Flattened earth spread
with stones, but no fire pit.
A hideout, a haven
for a desperate
or a brave person
to sleep in
on a dry night.

After the New Year's Eve chanting in church
for Armand

"Happy New Year," he said
to his friend.

His friend grinned and said,
"They say … that is,
the Buddhists say …
you have an inner awareness
and an outer awareness."
While speaking,
he raised his eyebrows
in questioning
and confirmation,
at the same time.

Then he lowered his eyebrows
and lifted them again
twice,
never blinking,
a contented smile on his face.

At that moment,
for that instant,
he got it –
or
it felt like he got it.

He nodded and smiled back at his friend.
Then they said goodnight
as a woman came up to his friend
eager to share the New Year's blessings.

Outside, rain poured down
freezing everywhere it touched earth.
He waited a moment then
stepped off the church stairs,
bent his knees and pushed off,
sliding down the slick sidewalk
like a six year old
finding himself wide awake at one
in the morning,
having more fun
than he'd ever had in the dark.

Faking it

for Amy

My problem she said,
in a passing moment of
introspection or
accidental revelation
while sipping a glass
of zinfandel, her favorite,
my problem is
I'm always celebrating life,
finding the happy ending.

If I don't know a book
will have a happy ending,
I can't read it. I like
to make people feel good, that
the best is possible. Not like
you, she said, you like the dark
stories where the sad and soulful
lose to the unredeemed. You like
indie films – I try them
but about 15 minutes in,

I have to change to something
funny, or at least romantic.
I know life is sorrowful,
of course it is, all artists know
that – and who's not an artist

whether they know it or not –
otherwise why bother with art?

It tries to make
you feel better, too,
doesn't it?

But I keep my misery to myself,
my own musing, I mean.
I hold my bad feelings private
and I keep a smile on my face.

She stood up
and straightened her shoulders.
Let's go out, she said,
let's find music someplace.
I need to hear people noise.
I want to see people smiling
and laughing, having a good time.

I don't care if they're faking it.

Love and sandwiches

for Paul Richmond
U.S. Beat Poet Laureate

A friend of mine
is a famous poet who says
"I'll work for sandwiches
but I wouldn't mind
making a little cash sometime."

We tell him
it's never too late.
You've only been a poet for 50 years,
famous for seven, maybe ten.

He's good
and getting better all the time.
He's real.
A humen spelling error
means nothing to him.
What matters are turtles
and music
and laughing.
He loves the people
who can feel the aches
and the anger
in his words.

Then when we start
to feel the lumps
in our throats,
he makes us laugh
and we feel safe.

"Do it now!" he sings,
showing his faith in us,
the same faith
that brought him fame
because he's the guy
who believes in us
and what we
can do.

Faith and love
don't make anyone real
any money
but if you have them,
you're as lucky
as if you traveled the world
carrying a picnic basket
always full of fresh sandwiches,
a poem to play with,
and now and then
on a chilly day,
a flask of coffee
to share with a friend.

Humid grace

You never know why
a blessing befalls you,
but you might notice the humid fragrance
of grace brushing your flesh from toe to head,
a silky drizzle warmer than tropical seas,
lighter than meadow breezes.

Your cells open to the caress,
cherishing the rill of excitement in your bones
as if an old friend had returned and,
delighted to see you,
slapped you on the back
and sent a shuddering wave of pleasure
across your chest.

Happy for no reason again,
you look up into the sun
and at that very instant your skin shivers.
A tickle of chill
balances the surge of warmth
from the sun and you're tempted to neigh or crow.

A cumulus cloud floats up
and you smile
and shake your head
in mock disbelief

and then it's pouring
those precipitant blessings
for the tenth day in a row,
the rain of fortune so dense
you can't see beyond the yard.
It soaks your clothes
and you don't care
and now what?

It's seventy-eight fahrenheit
and you have no excuse
not to go back to bed
and fool around all afternoon
with the one you love
who's already turning down the damp sheets.

TOGETHER

Logo for 2020 by Milton Glaser, New York, NY

Independence Day

In one of our last long hugs before you left,
    in this kitchen where we steamed
and broiled and blended and ate
    and broke plates and glasses
and rubbed against each other for years,

you bit my shoulder again and again.
    I gnawed and nuzzled your ear
catching hair in my teeth.
    Breeze from the empty park across the street
blew through our open front screen door,
    brushing our closed eyelids.

Outside, a boy carrying a stick
    fallen off one of the park's huge rock maples
strolled along a row of barrels
    the town set up to hold the trash expected
in the aftermath of tonight's Fourth of July fireworks.

He slapped a rolled steel barrel hard
    then gently stroked the next.
The barrels reverberated for a moment
    with the deep sound of a Buddhist gong struck,
mostly drum, some bell chime.

In the short silence between the barrels' thrums
    and children's voices calling from upstairs,
we let each other go and turned away
    to go on doing what we had to do
and I can't remember at all
    what that might have been.

Thinking to feel right

When we think too much,
ponder and propose logic
to others too often, it doesn't feel right

or kind to them, even when we know
we must think fast dancing thoughts
or slow crawling thoughts that do feel right.

There's no argument unless you think
there is. There's no thought unless you try
to say an idea that at the time feels right

and when it does, it seems it's either
no thought, like nothing, or a beautiful thought,
like a love poem. Nothing. Love. Both feel right.

Television night

Every night now is "television night"
Watching has something to do with shows
you don't want to fast forward the way

you have to hurry your life, from day to night
You give in to watch the TV,
and your sadness shows on your face
even though it glows the way

you would expect it to with the pale light
of false night and its stars far away from your chair.
It shows your wrinkles and smiles
as if you were traveling the ancient Way

while you watch TV, pretending the night
has nothing to do with how the shows
are magic, grab you, take you far away

Tommy, you thought you'd save the night
for dreaming or writing your own shows.
You still can if you stop using the clicker
to find your way.

Sad, glad

In this land of lawns gone back to scrub and dry,
longing for water inspires lovers with sadness.

Love inspires every other feeling,
even hate while we wait for rain, abiding in sadness.

Cool wind loses its crisp edge if it's dry.
If it's damp, we might moan with gladness.

Small world, we say, when we meet cousins
who flee melting glaciers flooding them with sadness.

Mornings now, Tommy, you wake a little nervous,
knowing your day will pass
in both sadness and gladness.

The dog's mind

The dog's mind was elsewhere.
Perhaps where the fox left
a juicy clump of musk
or where the twin mutts down the street
drop a rich beefy scent every day.
She was distracted.

Otherwise, why would she,
a being of urgency and beauty,
why would she
sit still
not even panting,
while he nattered on
with those people,
the neighbors,
who pretended
they liked him and her?

9 ways of being in 2020 in Sachsenhausen, outside Berlin

1.
We followed our escort,
a woman from California,
whose first job in Germany
five years ago
was guiding visitors around
the concentration camp.
Her favorite tourists were
an older gay couple
who were bicycling across Europe.

2.
A labor force –
expendable traitors,
cheap workers,
an endless supply
as long as the war lasted.

3.
Three weathered
six-foot tall
hanging posts
without crossbars
used to punish prisoners
for being themselves,
left in place,

leaned under the weight
of thousands of ghosts.

4.
Most of the buildings
in the camp
have been demolished.
Two have been rebuilt
as empty museums.

5.
Four flourishing maple trees
stand high
over reconstructed,
deserted prisoner barracks.
They were planted
not long after the camp
was abandoned
seventy some years ago.
Nearby, the parade ground,
dry empty earth
where living skeletons
and famous men
stood in icy winter
all night long
in roll call
until after twenty hours
they collapsed
and stayed down.

6.
The drains
in the floor
of the "infirmary."

7.
For two hours
we scuffed along
dusty paths
mostly in silence,
taking no pictures.

8.
All I could do
was find a small rock
and leave it
among others
on a granite slab.

9.
In the small groomed town
surrounding the camp,
lovely old stucco houses
with yellow flowers and pink bushes
in full bloom
in their green yards.

Holocaust Memorial, U.S. Embassy, Berlin, Germany

Friends

We have so many we love
and we don't see often.

Many of them
we don't share blood with
and the other good friends
we could see more often,
and if we did,
we might not know them
any better than
we know them now.

Those who talk
don't reveal much new
while the silent ones
well, we trust them
in a different way.

Friend,
break bread with me,
then let's tell stories,
any stories,
as long as we can,
as long as we want.
If you don't want
to talk on and on,

let's go
for a quiet walk
to decide not the fate
of the world,
but to be with each other
and decide when we'll see
each other again.

Why do people

Why do people enjoy hitting balls with sticks?
Why do people enjoy shooting guns?
Why do people forget their grandparents
except for the memory of the time
they slept in their cobwebby basement?

Is it because we have no answers that last
we pretend we know enough to carry us through
from dinner last night to the concert this weekend?

Because young people grow up too fast or too slow?

Because our to-do lists flutter into the recycling
before we cross off our tasks? Because we set goals
we're sure to miss?

Why do people ignore the ravaging storms coming,
their homeless neighbors and melted ice caps?
Do we really ignore the metal beasts
we can't see lurking on the edge of the city,
or do we just pretend it's all right
so we feel safe, at least for now,
believing it's always now?

Is it because we have hearts that feel
and eyes that see
but brains that find it hard to understand?

Why do people believe we're each unique?
Is it because of course we are
and in the long run,
when we pass beyond the horizon,
it may not matter anyway?
But, you wonder,
what if everything matters?

Brooklyn, early winter

Mohammed
around the corner
makes smoothies
for the children
and a bagel
with creamless cheese
for me.

With them
why should I worry.
More coffee, please.

Like others,
I hurry down the street
in bitter cold.
I feel strong
in my bald age,
and free,
the luckiest one
of all,
holding warm little hands
in mine.

That's it

I have friends who practice Buddhism.
I don't dispute their beliefs and practices
since we're Americans and
I was raised a Christian accepting
of all souls since everyone has a shot
at heaven, rising beyond, if not
our tearful human existence, one that comes to
an undeniable stop for everyone.

I don't know for sure but I think
Buddhists believes in the big nothing,
Christians the resurrection of the body,
Jews the truth, Taoism the yin/yang.
I'm ignorant about Islam, Hinduism, Paganism,
Shintoism, Rationalism,
and all the countless unnamed faiths.

What secrets do they know about
taking us out of this world of pain
and uncertainty, while here we are
breathing and talking and walking,
into a timeless world
of pure blessings or no pain at all
that most everyone seems to agree exists
out there, in here, somewhere, nowhere?

The faiths seem like fleets
of private spiritual airplanes
that pick up people
with special reservations
to cities beyond the maps,
transcendence some say,
ascension to the sublime,
to the who and what's behind, inside,
all over this life.

I've been around a while now and still don't get
it. I feel a bit sad
not to understand or have something
like that I can leave my kids
as my going away present.

The one thing I do know
that takes me out of this world,
rises me up even when I'm lying down,
is when my wife scratches and rubs
my bare back when we're half asleep.

I can't stay in this zone of have-to's and I'm
better-thans and uhohs
and watch where you're goings, buddy,
because her tender fingers send me
out of this, wild unpredictable one
into a reliable one of pure bliss.

To that you tell me, "We've come a longer way
than lying around grooming, old fella.
The fact is you only know how to be an ape!"
I say, "Yes. Yes. That's it!"

6-word stories

"For sale. Baby shoes. Never worn."
  Hemingway

Happiness alone is four flat tires.

Please, please.
I didn't mean to.

I'm not sad.
I'm just sleepy.

My house has thirteen doors.
Yours?

Come over at seven.
Bring wine.

Jimmy crack' corn.
I don't care.
Daylight savings time disappears.
SAD arrives.

Stop please.
That's enough.
That's nice.

Fire!
No, the maple trees' reflection.

Don't stay there.
Come on inside.

Black.
Yellow.
Brown.
White.
Dear friends.

That felt good.
Once more, please.

I told him he should go.

He's gruff. She's cross.
They're miserable.

I took my books to recycling.

Poverty.
Abuse.
Drugs.
Longing for love.

Warning: Border crossing.
Dreams become nightmares.

Sunset.
Bird chirps.
I whistle back.

Death would be her only
forgiveness.

I relax when you kiss me.

You're rich.
I'm curious.
She's free.

Smudged windows.
Gray sky.
Lonely boy.

That tastes so good.
More, please.

Blue sky. High clouds. Happy boy.

If you love me, why go?

What scares me is his heat.

My ancestors ate potatoes.
Yours, beef.

Section II Credo

So far

Last night I picked up a book
Took a good, long look
It was Bob Dylan words and sounds
They flew up and circled around
So far

They sang and they cheeped
They buzzed and they quacked
They said things deeper than deep
It wasn't truth that they lacked
So far

They said things older than old
Things today we forgot we were told
The sounds disappeared and when
His word flock took wing, off they went
So far

Then came coyotes with their pups
A couple of fox and a bobcat, too
I looked up
The sky was blue
So far

I called a friend
Who'd been out, was on the mend
We'd done some business together
Made it through some rough weather
So far

I said You got anything new
To tell me or say
I wish I did, he said, and blew
Real loud on his horn - Not today
So far

I opened the book, read some, said Wow
Heard my old-time favorite tunes
Saw death lurking in crumbling ruins
From back a while, it's happening now
So far

George, Eric, Brenda, Martin
Millions unnamed – women, girls, boys, men
We didn't expect a virus and all these tears
The killers sat down, sipping their beers
So far

It's so sad if the morning light
Didn't shine so damn bright
In the little children's eyes
Some of us would up and say goodbye
So far

Now don't think I'm going away
I feel a lotta love, not sure how it'll show
For you and you and more than I know
Bob Dylan words, good as ever, here to stay
So far

Section II Credo

Influences

Harriet Tubman confessed she was free
but no one was there to welcome her.

Yeats claimed you could have either
art or life, not both. Great writer, poor guy.

Galway Kinnell protected his poet's solitude
like a threatened mother bear.

Frederick Douglass made known
the common white fear that slaves
who could read would write
their own passes to freedom.

Hemingway despised adverbs but
what good did that do for him.

Eleanor Roosevelt told us to do things
we think we can't do.

Walt Whitman, wrestler of saplings
in the Pennsylvania woods
to restore his strength after a stroke,
proposed we bow down before no one
and dismiss all teaching
that claims it's the total truth.

Lao Tzu touted riding the qi dragon
and leaving the things of the world alone.

Andy Goldsworthy understands time
as art's essential medium.

Sojourner Truth reminded us
"Christ came from God and a woman.
Man had nothing to do with it."

Fred Rogers assured us helping others
was the most important thing we can do.

James Tate had his sources.

Alice Walker reminded us no body,
no thing, was created for anyone else.

James Baldwin defined love as a tough
and universal quest and daring and growth.

Karl Popper noted "All life
is problem solving."

Joe Evans said "Consider the tree."

Czeslaw Milosz saw eternal light
in everything on earth.

When Shirley Timmins died,
she died with a laugh on her lips.

Beliefs

Belief's original meanings of
'to love,'
'to prize,'
'to hold dear'.

Daydreams pouring into the vacuum
left by a lack of vision.

Fear disguised as a sense of responsibility.

Fear as an everyday walking companion.

Pain worth only as much as we can feel.

Fools and kings, roles we cherish.

Screen watching as absorbing
rejection and loss and emptiness.

Immersion in art as longing praised
and accepted as inevitable.

Loss as everyone's inheritance.

Doctrines as crutches.

Courage as the common
and sovereign talent
for human survival.

Belief in the future
of the blue and green world
and people taking care
replacing belief in a Supreme Being.

Poetry as an act of love.

Life force abides beyond
anything we can imagine.

Laughing as the supreme human gift.

The unknown and chance
as the mother and father of all.

Credo

"I believe."
"I commit myself."
"I engage myself."

I believe the imagination
is the human superpower.

I commit to love those I love
without conditions,
not hard to do
and rapturous in practice.

If I engage in dreams and love
and helping someone every day,
and if I play every day,
and if I bear suffering with patience,

I believe I will leave behind
on my pyre
an opus of good living
to drift away on the wind
until it reaches home
in the sea.

I believe in you.

I PLEDGE
ALLEGIANCE
to the

EARTH

and all the

LIFE

WHICH IT SUPPORTS.
ONE PLANET,
in our care, irreplaceable,
with SUSTENANCE and RESPECT
FOR ALL

www.ingramcontent.com/pod-product-compliance
Lightning Source LLC
Chambersburg PA
CBHW021935040426

42448CB00008B/1076